8/23

Celebrity Entrepreneurs

LADY GAGA

Amy Pettinella

Cavendish
Square

New York

Published in 2015 by Cavendish Square Publishing, LLC
243 5th Avenue, Suite 136, New York, NY 10016

Website: cavendishsq.com

This publication represents the opinions and views of the author based on his or her personal experience, knowle
and research. The information in this book serves as a general guide only. The author and publisher have used th
best efforts in preparing this book and disclaim liability rising directly or indirectly from the use and application
this book.

CPSIA Compliance Information: Batch #WW15CSQ

All websites were available and accurate when this book was sent to press.

Pettinella, Amy.
Lady Gaga / Amy Pettinella.
pages cm. — (Celebrity entrepreneurs)
Includes index.
ISBN 978-1-50260-036-3 (hardcover) ISBN 978-1-50260-037-0 (paperback) ISBN 978-1-50260-038-7 (ebook
1. Lady Gaga—Juvenile literature. 2. Singers—United States—Biography—Juvenile literature. I. Title.

ML3930.L13P48 2015
782.42164092—dc23
[B]

2014024956

Editor: Kristen Susienka
Copy Editor: Cynthia Roby
Art Director: Jeffrey Talbot
Designer: Joseph Macri
Senior Production Manager: Jennifer Ryder-Talbot
Production Editor: David McNamara
Photo Researcher: J8 Media

The photographs in this book are used by permission and through the courtesy of: Cover photo by Kevin Mazu
WireImage/Getty Images; Neil Mockford/FilmMagic/Getty Images, 4; Landov, 9; Marcaux/Photographer's Choic
Getty Images, 10; Chris Walter/WireImage/Getty Images, 12; Seth Poppel/Yearbook Library, 15; Herve GLOAGU
Gamma-Rapho/Getty Images, 17; Steve Granitz/WireImages/Getty Images, 18; Jacopo Raule/Getty Images, 21; R
Beck/AFP/Getty Images, 23; MATTHEW HEALEY/UPI/Landov, 25; Kevin Mazur/WireImage/Getty Images, 26
Gavan/Getty Images, 29; Stevenuccia/File:Guggenheim museum esterno.JPG/Wikimedia Commons, 31; Kevin C
WireImage/Getty Images, 33; JEFFREY R. STAAB/CBS/Landov, 34; Vladimir/File:Lady Gaga Sold Out at Rosel
Ballroom.jpg/Wikimedia Commons, 37; John Phillips/UK Press/Getty Images, 38; Gary Gershoff/WireImage/G
Images, 41.

Printed in the United States of America

CONTENTS

Lady Gaga: A Model of Success

How's this for a list of accomplishments? Lady Gaga has sold twenty-three million albums and sixty-four million singles, as well as won five **Grammy** awards and thirteen MTV Video awards. She was *Billboard Magazine*'s Artist of the Year, VH1's Fourth Greatest Woman of Music, one of *Time* magazine's Most Influential People in the World, and *Forbes* magazine's Most Powerful Celebrity in the World. She's done all this before her twenty-seventh birthday.

She is an entertainer, an artist, a fashion designer, an **entrepreneur**, and an activist. Perhaps "natural phenomenon" would be the best way to describe Lady Gaga. With the release of her first album, *The Fame*, at age twenty-two, she shot to the top of the music charts and into the hearts of her fans. Often dubbed the "voice of social outcasts," she is adored the world over for her generosity of spirit and playful personality.

As the songwriter, composer, and singer of some of the catchiest pop tunes the world has ever known, Lady Gaga consistently makes headlines. These days, those headlines are as much about her success as an entrepreneur as they are about her music career. During her brief career, Lady Gaga has earned the respect and admiration of some of the world's biggest corporations, such as Apple, for her ability to personally connect with her fans.

Many celebrities further their careers with product **endorsements**. Such business dealings are often as lucrative as their entertainment or sports careers. Gaga, however, is not content to simply appear in a magazine or television ad. She is an innovator. Some even call her an inventor. She has been known to inspire fantastic improvements on existing products, and to envision completely new ones. She is an artist, and what she loves to create more than anything is a feeling of "wonder."

Today, you can look to Lady Gaga as a role model for success. Even if you have no interest in pursuing show business, her approach to business is noteworthy. First and foremost, Lady Gaga is an extremely hard worker. From a young age, her parents taught her the value of a strong work ethic. Second, she is a visionary. When she has an idea, she shares it with other artists, designers, and businesspeople. She doesn't keep ideas to herself out of fear that they will not succeed or that others will make fun of her. If people suggest that her ideas are not possible, she responds, "Try anyway."

Lady Gaga's popularity is so enormous that some view her not just as a person but also as a brand. This branding has drawn the attention of large companies including Coca-Cola (Diet Coke is included in her touring contract **rider**) and Coty, Inc., with whom Gaga has a long-term licensing deal to create fragrances under her name.

To maintain their fan base, performers must establish a personal connection with their followers. How does Lady Gaga, someone who has sold more than two million concert tickets, personally interact with fans? She voices her adoration for them.

Gaga's fans perceive her adoration as genuine. "I want to be your cool older sister who you really feel connected with—who you feel really understands you and refuses to judge anything about you because she's been there," she says.

Her loyal fans buy every record, attend every concert, and watch every video or television special. They share her music and ideas with their friends, thereby encouraging more fans and supporters. Maybe you are one of them.

More than any other celebrity, Lady Gaga uses the draw of social media to sell her brand. Many celebrities create social media sites for self-promotion. Lady Gaga uses it to connect with her fans on a more personal level. It is not uncommon for her to reach out to a fan via social media to offer encouragement. Gaga inspired the creation of LittleMonsters.com, an online social community filled with art, acceptance, little monsters, and Gaga. There, her message and brand are promoted with frenzy.

Rarely does a pop star enjoy this level of brand loyalty. At just twenty-eight years old, Lady Gaga has experienced a remarkable journey to fame. In the seven years that have passed since the release of her first album, *The Fame*, Lady Gaga has undergone numerous transformations. Her ever-changing hair, makeup, and fashion statements are merely hints to the millions of ideas developing in her mind.

Business executives have courted Lady Gaga from the start, hoping to capture a spark of her incredible energy and imagination. She has inspired trends in music, fashion, technology, and perhaps most importantly, ideas about how people can make the world a kinder, braver place. Having faced more than her share of criticism, this is no small feat. Her history with people who criticize her, which started when she was bullied as a teenager, and her refusal to back down, inspires and encourages fans possibly experiencing similar obstacles in life. How did she become this sensation? Read on to find out.

Bullied as a teenager, Lady Gaga has inspired the awe and respect of fans and big businesses alike.

Stefani Germanotta spent her early years living in Manhattan's Upper West Side.

Chapter One

The World Is Her Stage

Stefani Joanne Angelina Germanotta was born on March 28, 1986, the firstborn of Cynthia and Joe Germanotta, who were living in Yonkers, New York. A **second-generation** Italian from a tight-knit and fun-loving family, Joe instilled in Stefani a strong work ethic and a sense of loyalty, to which Lady Gaga often credits her success. When Stefani was six years old, she welcomed little sister Natali. Shortly after Natali's birth, the family moved to Manhattan's Upper West Side.

The Germanottas' home was always filled with music. At age four, Stefani began taking classic piano lessons. Her parents exposed Stefani to classic rock stars, such as Bruce Springsteen and the Beatles, and New Wave performers, such as

Culture Club and Cyndi Lauper. Stefani, however, preferred seventies **glam rock** artists such as David Bowie and Queen. Dissatisfied with merely singing along to their records, she wanted to make music herself, to play the songs of Springsteen, the Beatles, and Elton John.

"When I was thirteen, my father … gave me a Bruce Springsteen songbook for the piano," Gaga recalls. "On it was 'Thunder Road.' My dad said, 'If you learn how to play this song, we will take out a loan for a baby grand.' It was the hardest thing to do … eventually I got it down." The piano today remains displayed in the Germanotta home.

Lady Gaga's style combination of pop and glamour was influenced by such iconic bands as Culture Club.

The Beginning and Growing Pains

Stefani was accidentally "discovered" when she was thirteen. While in a Manhattan clothing boutique, she had been singing along to a song on the radio when one of the employees there heard her. Impressed, he approached her, and recommended she contact his uncle, Donald Lawrence. Lawrence was a voice coach for many professional singers, including Mick Jagger and Christina Aguilera. Lawrence was impressed with Stefani's voice, and encouraged her to start writing songs. It wasn't long before Stefani began performing in coffeehouses and jazz clubs under her mother's supervision.

With a wealth of talent, a strong work ethic, and a home in a cultural mecca, it seemed that life was pretty good for Stefani. Outgoing and spontaneous, she loved to socialize, and was generally well liked for her infectious personality. As she grew into her teen years, however, relationships with her peers became more difficult.

Although the Germanottas worked hard to attain financial success, many of Stefani's classmates' families inherited theirs. Some of these classmates did not consider the Germanottas equals, and they often teased Stefani, who despised this modern-era **caste system**. In response, she expressed her individuality through unusual clothing and hairstyle choices. Stefani did her best to be bold during these times, which caused many to consider her a rebel. Ironically, her boldness and rebellion sometimes resulted in further bullying.

Rebellious streak aside, Stefani was a dedicated student who passionately pursued academics and the arts. As a student at the elite private school Sacred Heart, Stefani realized her parents had sacrificed a lot for her tuition. More than anything, she wanted to make them proud.

College and the School of Hard Knocks

At seventeen, Stefani was granted early admission to New York University Tisch School of the Arts. Majoring in performance arts, much of her coursework consisted of business classes. Stefani loved and excelled in these studies—a clue that she was a born entrepreneur. However, after spending a year at college, she announced to her parents she was leaving school.

Despite her parents' initial doubts about her chances of succeeding as a musician, Stefani's work ethic and artistic drive made them trust her decision. She set out on her own and landed on Manhattan's Lower East Side. The neighborhood, home to many DJs, singers, dancers, and musicians, promoted a **bohemian** lifestyle. Stefani began dancing and singing in clubs and making a name for herself. "[My dad] said, 'You have a year to make something happen or I'll make you go back to school.' But I wanted to live alone, live in solitude with my music, read poetry; be overly dramatic about everything. And I did."

Realizing that her image was also important, Stefani created a dynamic on- and offstage presence. She looked to long-gone idols Andy Warhol and Freddie Mercury for inspiration in

As a teenager, Lady Gaga enjoyed popularity for her personality, but also suffered bullying for her artistic expression.

this transformation. She meticulously studied how Warhol transformed stardom into an art form, and as a tribute to Queen's hit "Radio Gaga," she chose Lady Gaga as a stage name.

Soon after, she was signed by Island Def Jam—but was dropped before recording her first song. L.A. Reid, former president of Island Def Jam Music Group, admitted during a 2011 interview with *Access Hollywood* that he halted Lady Gaga's music pursuits: "I was having a bad day ... it was the worst thing I've ever done," he said.

A New Scene

In 2007, Stefani relocated to Los Angeles to be closer to the recording scene. Soon after, she was signed by Interscope Records, and in 2008 she composed *The Fame*, her first album. She was just twenty-two years old. An instant smash, the album sold more than a million copies and earned two **Grammy** awards.

Many companies, such as MAC Cosmetics, soon asked Lady Gaga to endorse their products. Being the face of a product suited her, but after a few successful endorsements, Gaga wanted to offer more. As the daughter of entrepreneurs, she was not interested in selling her name to the highest bidder. She was destined to be an entrepreneur herself.

Andy Warhol and The Factory

While living on the Lower East Side, Lady Gaga developed an obsession with Andy Warhol. Often credited with founding the pop art movement in the United States, Warhol was an influential American artist, author, and filmmaker who gained prominence in the 1960s. His work sparked a major cultural shift in how art was defined. Critics considered his work commercial and low class, but the general public thought it was genius. His famous paintings of soup cans fetched over $1,000 in 1962, but sold for $15 million in 1996. After his initial success as a painter, Warhol began collaborating with other artists, musicians, models, and writers in a warehouse in New York City known as The Factory, where they made numerous avant-garde films. Despite his enormous popularity, Warhol made several enemies on his path to fame, narrowly surviving an assassination attempt in 1968. He died in 1987 at the age of fifty-nine.

Lady Gaga in her famous meat dress at the MTV Video Music Awards in 2010.

Chapter Two

Pushing Boundaries

Lady Gaga is often considered the first **millennial** superstar. More than twenty million of her albums and sixty million digital downloads have been sold. She was the first artist to receive more than one billion hits on YouTube. Her success in blending pop art and lucrative business has drawn many comparisons to Andy Warhol. Along with her creative design crew, The Haus of Gaga, Lady Gaga continues to intrigue, inspire, and invigorate fans and the media.

Through her ability to grow her identity, Gaga has proven herself a master at marketing. Some business experts, such as *Forbes* magazine, which listed Lady Gaga as the highest-ranked newcomer on its 2010 Celebrity 100 list, and *Slate*, which dubbed Lady Gaga a "culturally and commercially dominant creative product," agree.

"Finally a Real Job" at Polaroid

Stefani was born at a time when communication technology was in its infancy. Few people had cell phones, personal computers, or Internet access. Perhaps it was the influence of her father, who was considered years ahead of his time when he launched an Internet company in the early 1990s, who spawned her interest in emerging technology. Her explorations into the technology world include partnerships with Apple, Zynga, and Polaroid.

In 2010, Polaroid approached Lady Gaga to help revitalize its product line. The company, launched in 1937, initially made sunglasses. By the 1970s, it was known as the company that introduced instant cameras. These cameras could produce fully developed photographs with the press of a button. By the early 2000s, however, most people were using digital cameras, and by 2008, Polaroid filed for **bankruptcy**. Hoping to revitalize its brand, the company reached out to Lady Gaga. Who better to reinvent their image than the queen of reinvention herself?

Gaga's initial line of products included a digital camera that could instantly develop pictures, a handheld wireless printer featuring a **patented** Zink (zero ink) technology, and the futuristic GL20 Camera Glasses. Working with a team of engineers, Lady Gaga helped envision, design, and develop these products. Her father was thrilled with this partnership, joking that she finally had "a real job."

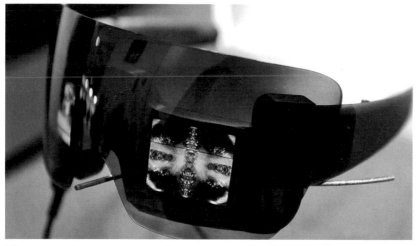

The GL20 Camera Glasses were designed to take pictures and movies, and to display them on the lenses for all the world to see.

LittleMonsters.com

Lady Gaga has long referred to her fans as her Little Monsters. In response, they call her Mother Monster. Gaga's fans hold a special place in her heart for always supporting her music, products, and her ideals about making the world a kinder place.

In 2010, while watching the movie *The Social Network* about Facebook founder Mark Zuckerberg, she was inspired to make her own mark on social media. At the time, she had millions of fans on both Facebook and Twitter. Lady Gaga wanted to provide her fans with a focused social media site on which they could personally connect to fellow Little Monsters and to Mother Monster herself. She approached her then-business manager Troy Carter, who was also somewhat of a tech guru, and LittleMonsters.com was hatched. Together, they enlisted **Silicon Valley** techies who started a new company called Backplane to create the network.

Littlemonsters.com launched in February 2012, the first social networking site of its kind. Lady Gaga encourages users to post their ideas for her brand, which she often uses, on the site. The platform has allowed Little Monsters to help create the brand, which reinforces their loyalty.

Fame: The Techie Perfume

Most people don't think of perfume as technology, but then again, most people don't think like Lady Gaga. In 2012, cosmetic company Coty teamed with Lady Gaga to create her first fragrance. Coty might have expected to send Gaga a few fragrance samples and bottle designs and take the reins from there. However, Lady Gaga had other ideas. She wanted her perfume to be "innovative" and instantly recognizable. Her conditions were that the perfume had to be black, and it had to turn clear when it hit the air. "They said 'no' for like a whole year," Gaga said of Coty's response to her ideas. "Even after I made the bottle so nice they said, 'We must just sell it as a regular perfume so you don't have to explain to everyone how it won't get on your clothing.' I said, 'I don't want to do it unless it's black.'" About the finished product Gaga stated, "You're not getting a random product that I signed off on. We really spent a lot of time creating this for you."

This double piano, created by The Haus of Gaga especially for Lady Gaga and Elton John, features the monster paw, the call sign of Little Monsters.

Fame perfume is presented in an egg-shaped bottle, which resembles the vessel from which she emerged at the Grammys to sing her hit "Born This Way." This bottle is adorned with the famous "monster paw," which is the greeting gesture for Little Monsters.

Lady Gaga, Activist: Born This Way

Even as a best-selling musician, successful entrepreneur, and one of *Forbes* magazine's Most Influential People in the World, Lady Gaga still wanted to do more. As a philanthropist, she'd donated millions of dollars for tsunami and earthquake relief in Japan and Haiti, and pledged $1 million to the American Red Cross to help with Hurricane Sandy relief in New York City. Yet there was still something missing. She wanted to give back to the people who gave her so much: her fans.

In 2011, Lady Gaga introduced the Born This Way Foundation. Its mission, according to its website, is to "foster a more accepting society, where differences are embraced and individuality is celebrated." Its launch at Harvard University in 2012 was a prestigious event and featured speeches by celebrities, such as Oprah Winfrey.

In 2012, Oprah Winfrey proudly championed Lady Gaga's Born This Way Foundation at the launch ceremony at Harvard University.

HAUS OF GAGA

The Haus of Gaga is Lady Gaga's team of fashion designers, videographers, hair and makeup artists, musicians, and set decorators. Her famous telephone hat, meat dress, and the egg—or "vessel," as The Haus prefers to call it—were all inspired, created, and built by The Haus. Much like Andy Warhol's Factory, The Haus works tirelessly to create her wardrobe, music videos, short films, and elaborate stages. The collective, as Lady Gaga likes to call the members of The Haus, was hand selected by Lady Gaga. Many of the artists were her companions when she lived on the Lower East Side, whom she trusts with her vision.

Chapter Three

Unlucky '13: A Year of Ups and Downs

Lady Gaga's parents, early on, taught her that she had to work hard at whatever she wanted to do: "In my house growing up … my parents instilled a very strong work ethic in me and my sister. As long as I worked hard at whatever I wanted to do, they were OK with me doing it." Gaga also loves what she does: "I live and breathe and love music and my art, and I'm a very passionate person, and I guess when you feel as though you will be empty without your work you don't mind the hustle and you don't mind stopping."

Tech Ventures

The Polaroid Grey Label products that Gaga helped design were a marvel of technology and creativity. "The Grey Label is my label,"

Gaga says. "I originally began working with Polaroid as a creative director and decided ultimately to create my own line of products that encompasses my dreams, my visions as an artist as well as the dreams and visions of Polaroid." The Grey Label products, she says, embody technology, fashion, and the digital era, as well as "the instant quality of the lifestyle of music, photography, and art, which is something that I'm obsessed with."

Just a few months after its 2012 launch, Gaga's social media product LittleMonsters.com boasted more than one million registered users, and over two million unregistered users. Apps for iPhone and Android use quickly followed the website's release and were highly profitable.

The key to any social media product's success is for the celebrity or company to use it as a personal connection tool, as Lady Gaga does. In addition to personally enlisting her fans to help promote her brand, Lady Gaga also offers special benefits, such as backstage passes, exclusive song downloads, and early ticket sales through the site, which gives them a reason to check in at least daily.

Lady Gaga's first **foray** into the fragrance market fared extremely well. Fame's release party, like Gaga's concert tours, was an extravagant ball. Held at New York City's prestigious Guggenheim Museum, hundreds of guests were invited to become a part of the **spectacle** by wearing wigs, masks, and hats. To unveil the product, a giant replica of the perfume bottle was on display. Inside the bottle, Lady Gaga, like Sleeping Beauty, slept on a **divan** where party guests could reach in and touch her hand. One week after its release, Gaga was delighted to share with her Twitter followers that over six million bottles had sold. Coty, the company that manufactured the fragrance, has since patented the amazing bottle technology innovated by Lady Gaga.

The Fame perfume bottle featured the famous Little Monster paw. It created a stir with its color-changing liquid.

Blood, Sweat, and Tears: Keeping the Brand Alive

When Lady Gaga stormed onto the scene in 2008, she toured and promoted relentlessly, enjoying meteoric success. This trend continued for more than five years, and it seemed that everything she touched turned to gold. By the end of 2013, however, it looked as if Gaga might have lost her **Midas touch**. For every good thing that happened, a bad experience, it seemed, followed.

Born This Way Ball

Lady Gaga's 2012/2013 Born This Way Ball tour had completed its Asia, Europe, and South America legs, and was on track to be one of the highest-grossing tours of all time. At the start of the North American leg of the tour, a hip injury forced Gaga to cancel the remaining twenty-one shows and refund the tickets sold. By some estimates, she lost more than $25 million in revenue. The cancellation of the tour seemed to be the start of a string of bad luck in both her professional and personal life.

ArtPOP or ArtFLOP?

Heartbroken at disappointing her fans with the concert cancellations, Lady Gaga used her recovery time to complete and promote her fourth album, *ARTPOP*. Two and a half years had passed since her last album, and fans were clamoring for new tunes. Like *Born This Way*, it debuted at number one, but record sales told a

Becoming an Art Exhibit: The Guggenheim

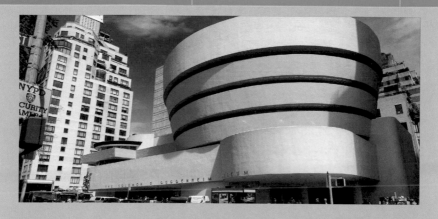

Despite moving to Los Angeles to launch her music career, Lady Gaga identifies herself as a New Yorker. She still considers the apartment she grew up in as home, and remains close to the friends she made when she lived on the Lower East Side. Gaga also identifies as being an artist rather than a singer: "I am a walking piece of art every day." When she launched her perfume at the world-renowned Solomon R. Guggenheim Museum in New York City, not surprisingly, Gaga's "Sleeping Beauty" performance was more of an art exhibit than a product launch. As a native New Yorker who has dedicated herself to the arts since the age of four, being an exhibit at the Guggenheim was a pivotal moment in Gaga's life. Take a virtual tour of the Guggenheim and learn about its impressive collection and history by visiting www.guggenheim.org.

different story. *Born This Way* sold over a million copies its first week. *ARTPOP* sold 285,000, according to *Billboard Magazine*. It did not help that her first single, "Applause," was illegally leaked to the public before its official release. A few days before the record went on sale, Lady Gaga and her longtime manager, Troy Carter, parted ways due to "creative differences," according to *Rolling Stone* magazine. Gaga seemed to take the brunt of the blame for the split. Perhaps the harsh media gossip that followed hurt her initial record sales, but by March 2014, the album had sold over two million copies. Such numbers represent success, not failure.

Still Inspiring Bravery: Born This Way Foundation

Canceled concert tours, management woes, and disappointing record sales did not discourage Lady Gaga's passion project, the Born This Way Foundation, or the companies that supported it. Office Max released a line of Born This Way back-to-school supplies, including "Kindness Sticks" Post-It Notes and gel bracelets, which bore the foundation's **tenets**: "Be Brave," "Be Amazing," "Be Yourself," "Be Kind," "Be Accepting," and "Be Involved." Through the sale of these products, Office Max donated more than $1 million to the foundation.

The foundation also launched its Born Brave Bus Tour, which traveled to scheduled concert cities. The bus, which is covered in artwork inspired by the Little Monsters, provides a fun, safe, and informative tailgate party to the general public. "At the Born Brave Bus you have access to professional private or group chats about mental health, bullying, school, and friends," said Lady Gaga via Twitter.

The Born Brave Bus gives Lady Gaga fans a chance to tailgate with concertgoers and learn more about the foundation.

Chapter Four

On the Edge of Glory

After the launch of her first album in 2008, Lady Gaga rose to the top of her game. In 2011, she sang about the thrill and fear of being "On the Edge of Glory." By 2013, however, parts of her world began to collapse. Gaga is a superstar, a woman known for her ability to overcome obstacles, but even Mother Monster is human. Like many, she struggles with personal and professional issues. She has admitted that the pace of her life "can be overwhelming" at times, and at one point she dubbed herself "a loser."

"Do I feel like a loser at times?" she asked. "Of course I do. We all do. I really feel misunderstood at times, but I celebrate my identity. I live halfway between fantasy and reality at all times. That is who I am."

Gaga, in 2013, openly discussed her bout with depression, describing it as "an anchor dragging everywhere I go." Her life as a superstar leaves her surrounded by many people, some with genuine interest in her life, others with negative agendas. In the past, Gaga says, "When I spotted someone with a hidden agenda, I allowed them to stay around me. I didn't want to believe it." Yet, she admits that she is now "better at not letting people take advantage of me."

However, Gaga did not climb to the top of the music world by having pity parties. She knew she had to move forward, to fight through the depression, to continue creating and evolving. "By January 1, I woke up … I looked in the mirror and said, 'I know you don't want to fight. I know you think you can't, but you've done this before … Whatever is left in there, even just one light molecule, you will find it and make it multiply.'"

Being one of the hardest-working women in pop "means that when you get knocked down, you pick yourself up and rub a little dirt in your wounds," Gaga has said. After a little downtime, she was refreshed, refocused, and redirecting her energy to new projects.

Roseland

For her twenty-eighth birthday, Lady Gaga threw a huge "funeral" bash at New York's legendary Roseland Ballroom, which closed its doors in April 2014. Many famous musicians performed at Roseland over the past century. New Yorkers were devastated about its impending doom, but were delighted that Lady Gaga would be the final performer. The seven-night concert gig was an instant sellout, so Lady Gaga offered free Internet streaming of the performance to New Yorkers and Little Monsters across the globe. Because her shows sell out regularly, most of her fans never get a chance to see her live.

Her seven-night residency in March 2014 at Roseland Ballroom in New York City ushered in newfound energy for Lady Gaga.

Lady Gaga often offers free streaming of her concerts when they sell out to ensure that her fans are rewarded. "They'll always stand by me and I'll always stand by them," says Gaga.

Undercover Fashion

Lady Gaga describes her personal style in one word: "free." It is often for this style that she is recognized. Her style also lends itself to her brand. Her array of theatrical outfits and accessories mark her as a unique character in the entertainment industry. Her signature pieces include hats. "They protect me in a different way. A social canopy, a hat is a social canopy. It is a nice barrier."

Lady Gaga is known for her bold fashion statements. Here she sits alongside hat designer Philip Treacy, wearing a flower piece he designed for her.

The bigger the better, Gaga says, and the more "interesting and outrageous the better. I always like when I have a hat that's big enough to keep people away at pretentious parties. It's protection. It's a sense of home away from home."

One of Lady Gaga's biggest supporters—and the designer behind most of the hats she wears—is Philip Treacy, a hat designer from London. He has referred to Gaga as his muse, and admits, "She's a really fun person to work with. She has a different sensibility—a different idea of what's perfect and beautiful."

Future Gaga

Some critics and tabloids often predict doom for Lady Gaga's career. She's had a few disappointing business ventures, and *ARTPOP* didn't sell as well as *Born This Way*. Yet these events hardly spell failure for the entertainer and entrepreneur.

As an entrepreneur, the products that reflect her signature style, such as her perfume with its monster paw, seem to fare better than those that don't. However, although her Polaroid career, for example, might have come and gone, Backplane is just getting off the ground. Gaga is considered by many to be a genius in marketing. Her uncanny skills have been the subject of best-selling business books and discussed in college courses. Possibly most satisfying is the continued success of her passion project, the Born This Way Foundation. Hundreds of thousands have boarded the Born Brave Bus during her worldwide tours.

Regarding future achievements, Lady Gaga says, "I hope to not be a celebrity. I hope I am perceived as separate from the idea of celebrity. I hope I am perceived as important, and loving, and peaceful, and enigmatic. I hope even more that I am perceived as good to my fans. I have so much to achieve ... I have artistically so much to say and so much to do." Musically, Gaga describes herself as "a garden and not a desert. I am so impossibly not finished. I always want to exist in a separate space—a Gaga space, a Monster space—that is impervious to anything else."

Lady Gaga says that she wants to be remembered as the superstar who "spread love with every attention." As for her Midas touch, perhaps that sentiment, as it pertains to Lady Gaga, should be: "Everything she touches turns to love."

Lady Gaga's loyal fans are often treated to a glimpse of the star before a concert.

Career Highlights Timeline

1986   Born in Yonkers, New York

1996   Moves to the Upper West Side

1997   Attends Academy of the Sacred Heart

2000   Begins singing career in coffeehouses and jazz clubs

2004   Graduates high school, attends NYU Tisch School of the Arts

2006   Leaves Tisch, moves to the Lower East Side

2007   Moves to Los Angeles, signs with and is dropped from Island Def Jam Music Group; signs with Interscope Records; starts touring as Lady Gaga

2008   Album *The Fame* released

2009   Album *The Fame Monster* released

2010   Named creative director at Polaroid

2011   Album *Born This Way* released

2012   Born This Way Foundation, Fame perfume, and littlemonsters.com launched; hip injury cancels tour

2013   Album *ARTPOP* released

Glossary

bankruptcy The financial collapse of a person, business, or organization.

bohemian A person who has informal and unconventional social habits, especially an artist or writer.

caste system A class structure that is determined by birth.

divan A bed that has a thick base and usually no footboard.

endorsements Public or official statements of support or approval.

entrepreneur A person who begins, organizes, and operates a business.

foray A first attempt at trying something new.

glam rock A style of rock music first popularized in the early 1970s, characterized by male performers wearing showy clothes and makeup.

Grammy Any of the annual awards given by the National Academy of Recording Arts & Sciences for special achievement in the recording industry.

Midas touch King Midas is remembered in Greek mythology for his ability to turn everything he touched with his hand into gold. A person with the "Midas touch" is said to have the gift of profiting from whatever he or she undertakes.

millennial A person who reached young adulthood around the year 2000.

patented The exclusive right granted by a government to an inventor to manufacture, use, or sell an invention for a certain number of years.

rider An addition to a document or contract.

second-generation The children of parents who have immigrated to a particular country.

Silicon Valley A nickname for the South Bay portion of the San Francisco Bay Area in Northern California, where there is a large concentration of technology firms.

spectacle Something that attracts attention because it is very unusual or very shocking.

tenets The main principles of a religion or philosophy.

Further Information

Books

Goodman, Lizzy. *Lady Gaga: Critical Mass Fashion*. New York, NY: St. Martin's Griffin, 2010.

Huba, Jackie. *Monster Loyalty: How Lady Gaga Turns Followers into Fanatics*. New York, NY: Portfolio/Penguin, 2013.

Lady Gaga, and Terry Richardson. *Lady Gaga*. New York, NY: Grand Central Publishing, 2011.

Marisco, Katie. *Lady Gaga: Pop Singer & Songwriter*. Minneapolis, MN: ABDO, 2012.

Websites

Born This Way Foundation
bornthiswayfoundation.org.
Check out the Born This Way Foundation and celebrate a more accepting society—one in which differences are embraced. Learn how you can get involved. Follow the Born Brave Bus Tour.

LadyGaga.com
www.ladygaga.com
Visit Lady Gaga's official website for news, music videos, concert updates, and music.

Little Monsters
littlemonsters.com
Connect with others, check out updates from Mother Monster, and enter contests on this social network for Lady Gaga fans.

Videos

"Lady Gaga: Inside the Outside"
youtube.com/watch?v=Gjt-EW3QGuk
Get up close and personal with Lady Gaga as she engages in an intimate conversation about life, family, music, ambition, high school, and more.

Lady Gaga on the *Oprah Winfrey Show*
"Born This Way" and "You & I"
www.youtube.com/watch?v=4HRSSTYwGMQ
Watch Lady Gaga performs hits from her album *Born This Way*.

Index

Page numbers in **boldface** are illustrations.

About the Author

Amy Pettinella is from Indianapolis, Indiana. By day she works in technology, but when the lights dim she is an author, music promoter, and playwright. She runs an intimate concert salon for international, national, and local indie artists and poets called the Beat Lounge. An active reporter of local arts and national music, she regularly reviews art and music for blogs *Mission Intrigue: Indy* and *No Depression Americana and Roots Music Authority*.